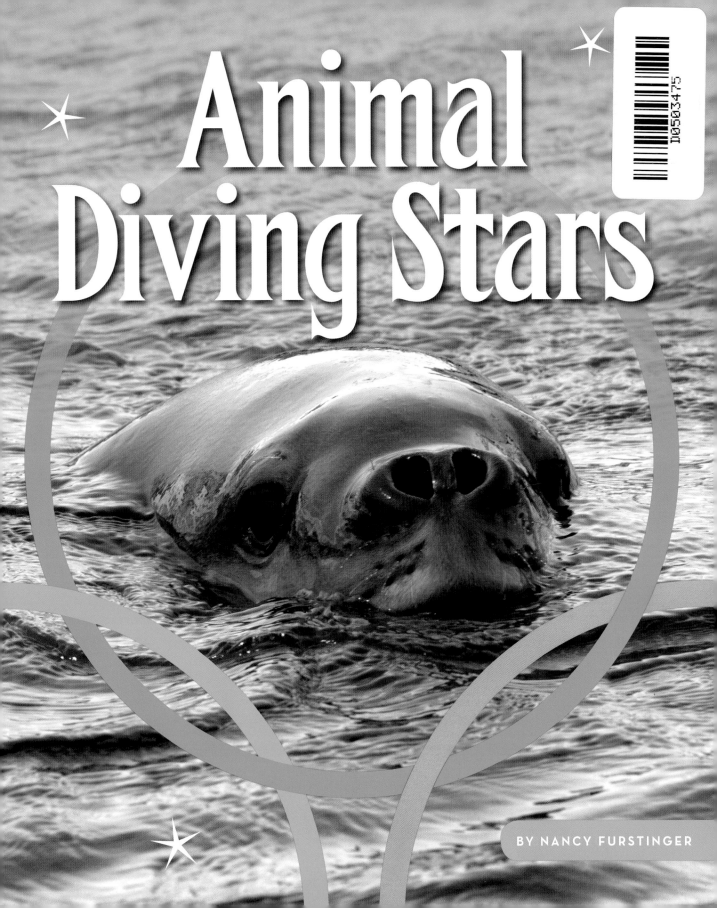

Animal Diving Stars

BY NANCY FURSTINGER

The Child's World®
childsworld.com

Published by The Child's World®
1980 Lookout Drive • Mankato, MN 56003-1705
800-599-READ • www.childsworld.com

Photographs ©: Dmytro Pylypenko/Shutterstock Images, cover, 1;
Animals Animals/SuperStock, 5; iStockphoto, 6; Britta Scherer/
Allstar/Sportsphoto Ltd./Allstar/Newscom, 7; Jo Crebbin/
Shutterstock Images, 9, 21; Nature Picture Library/Alamy, 10; Tui
De Roy/Minden Pictures/Newscom, 13; Todd Pusser/Nature Picture
Library/Alamy, 15, 20; D. Parer & E. Parer-Cook/Minden Pictures/
Newscom, 17, 20–21; David Osborn/Shutterstock Images, 18

ISBN 9781503820388
LCCN 2016960508

Printed in the United States of America
PA02341

ABOUT THE AUTHOR

Nancy Furstinger has been speaking up for animals since she learned to talk. She is the author of nearly 100 books, including many on her favorite topic: animals! She started her writing career in third grade, when her class performed a play she wrote while recovering from chicken pox. Since then, Nancy has been a feature writer for a daily newspaper, a managing editor of trade and consumer magazines, and an editor at two children's book publishing houses.

Contents

CHAPTER 1

Star Deep Divers

Imagine taking one breath that needs to last for minutes. Then imagine diving as deep into the ocean as possible. The animal kingdom is filled with athletes who are skillful divers. Which animals would win the gold, silver, and bronze medals if this were an Olympic competition?

Many animals can make extraordinary dives. What's their secret? They are strong swimmers. They have powerful lungs. These animals can lower their heart rate to help conserve oxygen. This is like having a built-in scuba tank. It allows them to dive deeper for a longer time. Could any human stand a chance against these animals?

Most animals that dive deep into the ocean are looking for food.

Some free divers aim to have the longest diving time. Others try to have the deepest dive.

Human free divers can also dive deep into the ocean. These athletes try to break world records. They swim without tanks or air. Instead, they use weighted sleds to dive down.

Free divers aim to go to depths of more than 650 feet (200 m). That is around the height of the Gateway Arch in St. Louis, Missouri! Computers record their depths.

On the way back up, divers **inflate** a balloon. This helps them get back to the surface quickly.

Herbert Nitsch is a free diving champ. He set a world record in 2007. That year, he dove 702 feet (214 m). In 2012, he smashed his previous record. Nitsch dove 830.8 feet (253.2 m). He holds more than 30 world records.

Nitsch has earned the title "The Deepest Man on Earth." But can he keep that title in a contest with the animal kingdom?

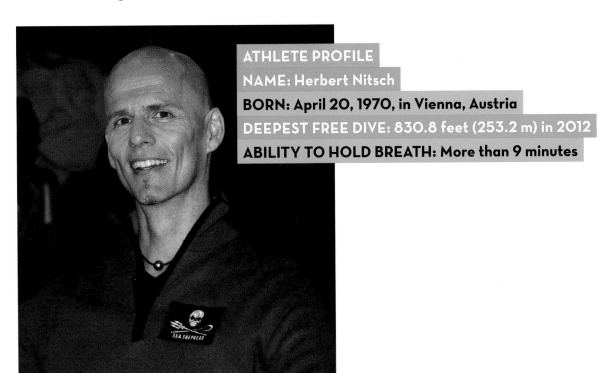

ATHLETE PROFILE
NAME: Herbert Nitsch
BORN: April 20, 1970, in Vienna, Austria
DEEPEST FREE DIVE: 830.8 feet (253.2 m) in 2012
ABILITY TO HOLD BREATH: More than 9 minutes

CHAPTER 2

Flying Birds Dive to New Depths

Many birds soar to dizzying heights in the air. Some seabirds, such as penguins, descend to new depths below the sea. One bird, however, holds the diving record for flying birds. That bird is the thick-billed murre.

ANIMAL PROFILE
NAME: Thick-Billed Murre (MER)
LENGTH: 18 inches (46 cm) long
WEIGHT: 25 to 52 ounces (709 to 1,474 g)
DEEPEST DIVE: 690 feet (210 m)

The thick-billed murre is better at diving than it is at flying. But it can still fly at nearly 75 miles per hour (120 km/h).

The thick-billed murre can live up to 25 years.

The thick-billed murre is a deep-diving champ. These flying birds plunge down at least 330 feet (100 m) in the water. The record-holding murre more than doubled this dive. It dove 690 feet (210 m) below the water.

Thick-billed murres use their wings to race through the water. They can reach speeds of 6.5 feet (2 m) per second. They can stay underwater for three minutes. Then, after resting for less than a minute at the surface, the birds are ready to dive again. They can dive up to 20 times in a row.

Why is this bird so determined? The answer is food. The thick-billed murre dives down to grab **prey**. It swallows fish and squid below the sea.

The bird hunts for prey in Arctic waters. Each summer, it nests on ledges of sea cliffs. In winter, the thick-billed murre **migrates**. It swims to waters off the coast of Canada and New England.

CHAPTER 3

Beaked Whales Set Records

Whales are famous for holding their breath underwater. They can do this for a long time. But one whale species has broken two dive records.

Scientists put **satellite tags** on Cuvier's beaked whales. Then, they tracked these small whales off the coast of California. One whale stayed underwater for 138 minutes! It set a record for marine mammals.

Another whale in the same group also set a record. This one was for deep diving. The data stunned scientists.

ANIMAL PROFILE
NAME: Cuvier's (KOO-vee-ays) Beaked Whale
LENGTH: 15 to 25 feet (4 to 8 m) long
WEIGHT: Up to 7,000 pounds (3,175 kg)
DEEPEST DIVE: 9,816 feet (2,992 m)

It's rare to spot these whales out at sea.

The Cuvier's beaked whale had dived nearly 10,000 feet (3,048 m).

How do these whales dive so deep for so long? They have bodies built for deep-sea diving. Whales can collapse, or deflate, both their rib cage and lungs. This allows them to withstand water pressure at lower depths. Whales also exhale most of the air in their lungs before they dive. This helps prevent them from floating. It makes it easier to dive.

The Cuvier's beaked whale can be found in oceans at least 3,300 feet (1,006 m) deep. Like other toothed whales, they use clicking sounds to hunt for prey. The clicks echo back from the whales' favorite meal: squid.

The Cuvier's beaked whale is also called the goose-beaked whale.

CHAPTER 4

Plunging Southern Elephant Seals

Southern elephant seals spend most of their lives in chilly Antarctic waters. Up to 90 percent of that time is spent underwater. They dive around the clock.

These seals start off huge. Most pups are born weighing around 100 to 110 pounds (40 to 50 kg). Soon after the pups are born, the mothers leave.

ANIMAL PROFILE
NAME: Southern Elephant Seal
LENGTH: Up to 20 feet (6 m) long
WEIGHT: Up to 8,500 pounds (3,856 kg)
DEEPEST DIVE: 4,921 feet (1,500 m)

Elephant seals go to shore only twice a year, in the summer and winter.

The southern elephant seal is the largest seal in the world.

The pups have to master swimming and diving if they want meals.

Scientists have studied southern elephant seals. They have recorded how deep the seals can dive.

One seal dove nearly 5,000 feet (1,524 m).

These seals can dive for a long time, too. They lower their heart rate to a single beat per minute. This lets them stay under the sea for up to two hours!

There, the hunt is on. Seals use their whiskers to sense nearby movement to locate prey. They swim in freezing cold water. Seals have a thick coat of blubber that keeps them warm. Why do they stay in these icy seas? That's where their food is found! These seals feast on fish and squid. Then, they bob back to the surface. They breathe above water for two to three minutes before plunging back down.

Fun Fact

Southern elephant seals do not get their name because of their huge size. They are named for their inflatable noses. Adult males blow up their snouts, so they look like elephant trunks. Then, they use them to make roaring noises that attract females.

CHAPTER 5

The Award Ceremony

GOLD MEDAL
Cuvier's Beaked Whale

SILVER MEDAL
Southern Elephant Seal

The gold medal goes to the Cuvier's beaked whale! This whale broke records when it dove 9,816 feet (2,992 m). It also held its breath for 138 minutes. The silver medal goes to the southern elephant seal. The thick-billed murre wins the bronze medal. Congratulations to all of these animal divers!

BRONZE MEDAL
Thick-billed Murre

Glossary

inflate (in-FLATE) To inflate is to add air or gas to something to make it larger. Deep divers inflate a balloon to help them get back up to the surface.

migrates (MYE-grates) Animals that migrate move from one region to another at different times of the year. The thick-billed murre migrates in the winter to find food.

prey (PRAY) Prey are animals that are hunted by another for food. The thick-billed murre grabs prey from the air.

satellite tags (SAT-uh-lite TAGS) Satellite tags are special chips that are attached to animals and used to track the animals' movements. Scientists use satellite tags to monitor Cuvier's beaked whales.

To Learn More

In the Library

Alderfer, Jonathan K. *National Geographic Kids Bird Guide of North America*. Washington, DC: National Geographic, 2013.

Kratt, Martin and Chris Kratt. *Wild Sea Creatures: Sharks, Whales, and Dolphins!* New York, NY: Random House, 2014.

Owings, Lisa. *Elephant Seal*. Minneapolis, MN: Bellwether Media, 2014.

On the Web

Visit our Web site for links about animals that dive: childsworld.com/links

Note to Parents, Teachers, and Librarians: We routinely verify our Web links to make sure they are safe and active sites. So encourage your readers to check them out!

Index